D0116362

TREASURES FROM THE PAST

TREASURES FROM ITALY

David & Patricia Armentrout

The Rourke Book Company, Inc.
Vero Beach, Florida 32964

PHOTO CREDITS:
©William Hammer: cover, pages 37, 41; ©Susan Alworth: pages 11, 23, 26; ©Al Michaud: pages 6, 16,
24, 29, 30, 33; ©Galyn C. Hammond: pages 18, 42; ©Anthony R. Dalton: page 27; ©Corel Corporation:
pages 15, 19, 32; ©University of Cincinnati/University of Tübingen: page 20; ©Artville, LLC.: page 4

PRODUCED & DESIGNED by East Coast Studios
eastcoaststudios.com

EDITORIAL SERVICES:
Pamela Schroeder

Library of Congress Cataloging-in-Publication Data

Armentrout, David, 1962-
    Italy : treasures from the past / David and Patricia Armentrout.
        p. cm. — (Treasures from the past)
    Includes index.
    ISBN 1-55916-292-9
    1. Italy—Antiquities—Juvenile literature. 2. Excavations (Archaeology)—Italy—Juvenile literature. [1. Italy—Antiquities.
2. Archaeology.] I. Armentrout, Patricia, 1960- II. Title. III. Treasures from the past (Vero Beach, Fla.)

DG77 .A73 2000
937—dc21

                                                        00–029077

Printed in the USA

TABLE OF CONTENTS

THE ROMAN EMPIRE
1ST century BC – 3rd century AD

ROME

CHAPTER 1

VALUE AND TREASURE

How do you define treasure? Is treasure made of gold, silver, diamonds or emeralds? Is treasure coins and jewelry?

Treasure to one person may not be treasure to another. Something "treasured" is something that is valued. People value different things for different reasons.

Maybe you value your CD or video collection. Maybe you value an antique doll or a watch your grandfather passed on to you. Love letters written by **ancestors** who have passed away are family treasures. There are many treasures in the world. They come in all shapes and sizes and are made from all kinds of materials.

Try to imagine what people treasured 100 or 1,000 years ago. They didn't have music CDs! They may have had money, or jewels, or even special toys, but they did not have a lot of what we have today. Ancient people lived a very different life.

Giant stone pieces were once part of an Emporer Constantine statue. They are remains from the Classical Roman period.

TIMELINE

753 BC	Legendary finding of Rome by Romulus and Remus.
753 – 500 BC	Rome is ruled by Etruscan Kings.
500 – 31 BC	Rome is ruled by a republic government. Etruscan rule ends.
400 BC	First Roman coins are made.
48 BC	Caesar defeats Pompey. Pompey is murdered.
44 BC	Caesar is murdered.
31 BC – AD 476	Roman Empire controls Rome and much of the land surrounding the Mediterranean Sea. Forum buildings and arches are constructed throughout this period.
27 BC	Augustus is first Emperor of Rome.
AD 69	Construction of the Colosseum begins. Vespasian is Emperor.
AD 79	Mt. Vesuvius erupts and destroys Herculaneum and Pompeii. Vespasian's son Titus is Emperor.
AD 118	Pantheon construction begins. Hadrian is Emperor.
AD 300 – 400	The Empire splits in two. The center of the empire moves east towards Asia.

How can we learn about ancient people's lives and what they valued? There are scientists who study past life. An **archaeologist** learns about past life by studying remains from long ago. Archaeologists and other special scientists try to figure out what people were like in the past. They want to learn how ancient people lived—how they worked, played, and died.

Archaeologists have many ways to study past life. One way is to read written records from a past civilization. Anything that has been written down is recorded history. Of course, there is **evidence** of past life before written records. The time before people used writing is called pre-history. If there is no recorded history, then scientists are left with bones and objects, called **artifacts**, to study. Artifacts can be manmade tools, bowls or jars, coins, jewelry, and even large objects like buildings.

Archaeologists study written records and artifacts to learn about past civilizations. Some of the artifacts may, or may not, have been treasures to those who used them. However, they all are treasures to today's archaeologists.

Archaeologists find hundreds of pieces of pottery, but they don't discard them. They spend days, even weeks, putting together a clay pot in search of clues to past life.

DISCOVERING PAST TREASURES

Treasure comes in many forms. It is important to know, too, that there are many kinds of archaeology. Some archaeologists study only some areas of the world, and some study only some time periods.

A **Paleolithic** archaeologist studies the time period before metals were discovered. The Paleolithic period, or Old Stone Age, began over 2 million years ago. Some archaeologists study more recent times like the **Mesolithic** period, and some scientists study present-day civilizations.

An Egyptologist is an archaeologist who studies ancient Egypt. Classical archaeologists study ancient Greece and Rome. This books deals with classical archaeology.

Rome and other areas in Italy were **inhabited** before 753 BC. Archaeologists have **excavated** many parts of Italy and Sicily and have found stone tools and weapons, and pottery pieces, called shards, that date back thousands of years. However, the city of Rome was founded, according to legend, in 753 BC. Early Roman civilizations affected how Italy and other nearby countries developed.

How do archaeologists discover these pieces of evidence? Sometimes artifacts are found by accident. Archaeologists might then decide to excavate the area. Other times archaeologists find information from written records and use it to find a **dig** site.

Once a site is chosen to research, scientists collect materials they need for the job. They use tools like shovels, buckets, measuring tapes, picks, and brushes at sites. The small hand tools and brushes help them remove soil from tiny pieces of evidence like fossils and bones. Archaeologists also put soil through a **sieve** to catch very small items.

*T*he Colosseum's real name is the Flavian Amphitheater.
Much of it still stands even though it was damaged in several earthquakes.

Ancient buildings are also a good place to begin excavation and research. Italy has many buildings from the time of ancient Rome. Archaeologists ask themselves, "How old are these artifacts?" Scientists use **chronology** and written records from past civilizations to find out how old things are.

Chronology is a science that places items and events in order. Chronology is a very detailed science. Scientists first use "relative dating" to separate items into younger and older categories. "Absolute dating" is how they find the exact age of an item. The details of dating items can be hard to understand for those who know nothing about it. Fortunately, we have well-educated scientists who can help us learn when and how ancient people lived.

EARLY ROMAN INFLUENCES

Archaeologists use chronology to date artifacts found in Italy. Dating the artifacts shows them how the cultures changed over time. Some artifacts, such as stone tools and weapons, date from about 5000 BC. Others items made with wood and bronze date from about 2000 BC. Iron artifacts date from about 1000 BC. As the centuries passed, the cultures in Italy became better educated and improved their skills. Each past culture helped build later civilizations.

The Etruscans *(ee TRUHS kuhnz)* were an ancient culture that lived in central Italy from about the 8th century BC. The Etruscans were skilled in building bridges, canals, and **temples.** Archaeologists have not been able to excavate many Etruscan cities because they are buried under newer cities. They have learned about the ancient culture by studying Etruscan **tombs.**

It was **tradition** for the Etruscans to build, or carve from rock, a "city of the dead." The city of the dead was a collection of tombs in an area just outside an Etruscan town. The tombs have many fine examples of Etruscan art. The artifacts found in the tombs include bronze statues, vases, lamps, and beautiful gold jewelry. The jewelry pieces include bracelets and necklaces that are quite fancy.

Early Rome was ruled by Etruscan kings, but around 500 BC the Etruscan rule fell to a new government. The new government was a republic run by elected men. During the republic years, Rome grew. Battles for land and Roman power continued for years.

Archaeologists have found many colorful paintings in Etruscan tombs.

Marcus Aurelis was emperor of Rome from AD 161 - 180.

One of the last great fights for Roman power was between Julius Caesar *(SEE zur)* and Pompey *(PAHM pee)* the Great. Each had their own army. Caesar defeated Pompey many times. Pompey fled to Egypt in 48 BC and was later murdered there. Caesar followed Pompey to Egypt and got involved in Egypt's civil war. Under Caesar's rule, Rome controlled Italy, Spain, Greece, Egypt, other European and North African areas, and most of the Mediterranean islands.

Rome changed from a republic government to the powerful Roman Empire in 31 BC. An empire is a large group of states ruled by one person—the emperor. The Roman Empire's boundaries were much larger than Italy today. The empire lasted in Rome until 476 AD. It lasted longer in regions far away. The Middle Ages describes the years after the fall of the Roman Empire.

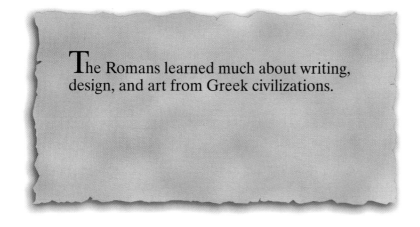

The Romans learned much about writing, design, and art from Greek civilizations.

Imagine the different cultures that were brought together through travel and trade in ancient Rome. The Romans were influenced by many cultures, but the Etruscans and the Greeks influenced Roman style the most. Roman bridges show Etruscan skill. Some Roman buildings display Greek styles. It is easy to understand why classical archaeologists study both ancient Greece and Rome.

Even though the Romans adopted styles from other cultures, they did create styles of their own. The dome and the use of huge arches are two examples of Roman building style.

Trajan was emperor of Rome from AD 98 - 117. Trajan built the largest forum in Rome.

A chariot race is painted on this Etruscan vase.
Chariot racing in ancient Rome took place at the Circus Maximus.

Archaeologists clean an ancient Roman mosaic floor.

ROMAN BUILDINGS

Some structures hold up well over hundreds of years. Have you ever wondered why? It is because of the materials and how they are put together. Structures last longer if they are strong and not damaged by weather or people.

Romans worked with many types of building materials. They used mud bricks and wood timbers in their earlier structures. Then they began to use clay bricks that were fired. Fired bricks arc stronger than mud bricks. They also used limestone and invented a strong cement. Romans also used marble, a very strong stone. Marble was saved for important structures like temples and court houses, and it was carved into beautiful sculptures.

Archaeologists have been working in many areas where they've found ancient Roman buildings. They have been studying the materials used in those buildings. The studies are part of "The Imperial Forum Project," which began in the 1990s. The project allows archaeologists to excavate buildings built during the Roman Empire. At the digs, scientists look for things that show natural **decay** or human destruction. They have learned that if holes in a building foundation are empty, then someone has taken something. Some of the sites in the project are now open to the public. You can visit many other ancient Roman ruins as well.

Arches in ancient Roman buildings were decorative and functional.

*P*alatine Hill lies east of the forum remains.

The Roman Forum

Forum is a Latin word that means "market place." Rome's forum was located in the heart of the city on a low-lying piece of land about 300 feet (91 m) long and 200 feet (60 m) wide. Three hills, the Capitoline *(KAP it uh lyn),* the Palatine *(PAL uh ten),* and the Esquiline *(EHS kwuh lyn),* overlooked the forum. The forum was made up of buildings used for business. It was the place where government officials came to work each day. The forum was lined with markets, temples, and **basilicas**. A basilica was a huge long hall used as a court of law. The name "basilica" was also given to important Roman churches.

As the Roman government changed from a kingship to a republic to an empire, the forum changed, too. The buildings got bigger and grander in style. As new emperors gained power, they added buildings to the forum. The remains of the Roman forum today are made up of six forums—the first, and the additions built by emperors Caesar, Augustus *(uh GUHS tuhs),* Vespasian *(ves PAYZ ee uhn),* Nerva *(NER vuh),* and Trajan *(TRAY juhn).*

Ruins of ancient Roman structures remain in such places as Morocco, Turkey, Libya, Algeria, Greece, France, and England—all past parts of the Roman Empire.

In the late 1800s excavations of the forum showed that many parts had been destroyed and then rebuilt, or built upon with newer materials. One dig took place on a slope of Palatine Hill. Digging down several feet, scientists found a piece of a wall. An archaeologist who studies soil and rock examined it. The scientists believed they uncovered a wall from the first forum built in the 7th century BC.

The ancient Roman Forum is always being studied by archaeologists.

*M*odern Rome was built around the ruins of the ancient Roman Forum.

The oldest section of the forum lies on its western edge. Little evidence remains of the Temple of Vesta, the Temple of Castor and Pollux, or the senate house. A senate house, or curia, was the building where members of the senate made important decisions about the government. Temples were places for worshiping gods, but were also used for military ceremonies. Other remains of the ancient Roman Forum include the Basilica Nova, the Temple of Venus and Rome, and structures from the emperors' forums.

The Pantheon

The Pantheon *(PAN thee ahn)* was built by emperor Hadrian *(HAY dree uhn)* about AD 118. More than 1,800 years old, the Pantheon is still whole. It is one of the best preserved Roman buildings. The Pantheon is a round temple covered by a dome. The dome and the round drum-shaped wall are solid concrete. The drum wall is 20 feet (6.1 m) thick, but it has hollow areas. In AD 609 the Pantheon was made into a church, which has protected it from looting and destruction.

*S*tone was taken from the Colosseum during the Middle Ages.
It was used to help build St. Peter's Basilica.

Romans used marble in many of the forum buildings.

Other structures designed by Hadrian include his villa, or home, near Rome, and Hadrian's Wall in England. The villa ruins run across 600 acres (243 ha). Pavilions, baths, libraries, fountains, and a stadium were once part of his home. You can see sections of Hadrian's Wall in northern England. At one time the stone wall was over 73 miles (118 km) long. It was used to help keep attackers at bay while Roman troops prepared to fight back.

Aqueducts and Bath Houses

The Romans were very picky about the water they used for drinking and bathing. Staying healthy and clean was important to them so they invented a sewer and **aqueduct** system. Designed by engineers, the aqueducts moved water from one place to another. They provided water to the major cities of the Roman Empire.

Early aqueducts ran mostly underground. They were made of pipes and stone-lined ditches. Later aqueducts had canals supported by arched walls or bridges. They stood high above gorges, rivers, and city buildings. Romans used concrete and stone to build them. Water ran through stone and clay pipes and tunnels. The aqueducts had siphons, filters, and storage tanks. Some moved water more than 50 miles (80 km). Rome's water system was so large it had 11 aqueducts 298 miles (479 km) long.

The aqueducts were a smart way to bring fresh water from the hills to a city's fountains, homes, and public bath houses. Large sewer tunnels below ground carried dirty water away from cities and into nearby rivers. Roman aqueducts still remain in many sections of Italy and across Europe. The famous *Pont du Gard* aqueduct in Nimes, France, is one of the remaining Roman structures in the area. It was built in 19 BC.

A furnace was used to heat a boiler that supplied hot water to Roman bath houses.

The Pont du Gard *Roman aqueduct was built in 19 BC.*
It is located just outside the Nimes city limits in France.

33

Much of the water brought into Roman cities went to the hundreds of Roman bath houses. A bath house was used for social gathering, exercise, and relaxation. The bath houses were large buildings divided into sections. Romans used gymnasiums for exercise. Other areas had hot, warm, and cold tubs for bathing. Romans could get oil massages in other sections. Many of the houses had large courtyards and gardens. Men and women used the baths at separate times of the day.

Many Roman bath houses had attached rooms with public toilets. Fifty or more people could do their "business" while chatting about the day's weather!

CHAPTER 5

ROMAN ENTERTAINMENT

Circus Maximus

The Circus Maximus was the Roman racetrack where **chariot** races took place. Chariots were open carts on two or four wheels. The driver, called the charioteer, drove horses that were hooked up to the chariot. Several teams of horses raced at the same time around the long oval track. The first chariot to cross the finish line won and the charioteer brought home gold for his efforts.

Chariot racing drew a big crowd. It was an exciting event. Spectators were able to bet on and cheer for their favorite team. They also bought refreshments from local vendors.

Colosseum

The Colosseum was an ancient Roman **amphitheater.** It was named for a colossal, or huge, statue nearby. The statue is no longer there. Construction on the Colosseum began in AD 69 during the reign of Emperor Vespasian. It was completed in the year 80 under the rule of Titus.

The remains of the Colosseum are at the east end of the forum in Rome. Unfortunately, you can no longer see the beautiful workmanship of the ancient Romans. Sections of the Colosseum have been destroyed in earthquakes. Ancient people also took stone from the Colosseum for other buildings.

When it opened, the Colosseum stood 160 feet (49 m) tall and could hold 50,000 people. The top of the Colosseum once had tall wooden poles that held a covering in place to keep spectators out of the sun. The outside wall had four levels that were supported by many arches.

Rooms below the Colosseum's floor held animals such as lions and elephants.

Spectators entered the Colosseum through 80 arched entry ways at the bottom level. Inside were rows of seating. In the center was a wooden floor covered in sand. Brutal battles between **gladiators** took place on the sandy floor. A gladiator was a trained fighter. Some gladiators were slaves, others were prisoners, and still others were volunteers. They fought bloody battles, many times to the death. The ancient Romans were not bothered by the violence and blood. They were very entertained by the event.

Gladiators and other men also fought wild animals in the Colosseum. The animals stayed below the arena floor in pens. Before the fight, they were raised to the arena level by an elevator.

When the bloody gladiator battles were not enough, the emperor removed the Colosseum floor and flooded the arena with water. This turned the arena into a "sea" where gladiators fought each other in small ships.

CHAPTER 6

BURIED CITIES

More than 100 miles from the ancient Roman capital is a very interesting place for archaeologists. It is a piece of land at the base of Mt. Vesuvius *(vuh SOO vee uhs)*.

Vesuvius is a volcano that rises about 4,200 feet (1,280 m) from the Bay of Naples. Vesuvius is an active volcano. It has erupted several times in the past few hundred years. Scientists are always studying this volcano. It is not what may happen in the future that interests archaeologists. It is the eruption of AD 79 that keeps them coming back for more.

On August 24th Vesuvius erupted. The eruption didn't stop until the next day. In the path of the lava flow, ash, and deadly gases, were a few small towns and two larger cities, Pompeii *(pohm PAY)* and Herculaneum *(her kyoo LAYN ee um)*. People who fled the cities wrote their stories down in great detail. Others who watched the horrible event from across the bay did the same.

Lava and ash destroyed Pompeii and Herculaneum. More than 2,000 people died at Pompeii. The city was covered in 20 feet (6 m) of volcanic ash and rock. Herculaneum was covered with a layer of hot mud 65 feet (20m) deep. The mud poured into the streets and into homes and businesses. Surprisingly, most of the people of Herculaneum were able to escape the boiling mud flow.

Mt. Vesuvius is 8 miles from the ruins of Pompeii's forum.

Archaeologists made plaster casts from holes in the dried volcanic ash.

The buried city of Herculaneum was discovered in 1709. Excavations began a few years later. Scientists found evidence of paved streets and sidewalks. In the hardened mud were complete buildings including a basilica, a theater, and the forum in the town's center. Archaeologists uncovered murals and **mosaic** walls and floors in a house that dates back to the 3rd century BC.

In 1860, an archaeologist at Pompeii noticed holes in the dried ash. He poured plaster into the holes to make molds. The dried plaster formed casts of bodies. Archaeologists could see exactly how the bodies lay at the moment of death.

Today more than half of Pompeii has been uncovered. The ruins show a city that was once oval-shaped and surrounded by a wall with towers and gates. Visitors can walk the streets and see rebuilt fountains, a temple, a marketplace, a courthouse, and renewed gardens with trees and flowers.

PLACES AND NAMES PRONUNCIATION GUIDE

Places:

Capitoline	*(KAP it uh lyn)*
Esquiline	*(EHS kwuh lyn)*
Herculaneum	*(her kyoo LAYN ee um)*
Vesuvius	*(vuh SOO vee uhs)*
Pantheon	*(PAN thee ahn)*
Palatine	*(PAL uh ten)*
Pompeii	*(pohm PAY)*

People:

Augustus	*(uh GUHS tuhs)*
Caesar	*(SEE zur)*
Etruscans	*(ee TRUHS kuhnz)*
Hadrian	*(HAY dree uhn)*
Nerva	*(NER vuh)*
Pompey	*(PAHM pee)*
Trajan	*(TRAY juhn)*
Vespasian	*(ves PAYZ ee uhn)*

GLOSSARY

amphitheater (AM feh THEE eh ter) — an oval or circular structure that has rising layers of seats around an arena, like today's sports stadiums

ancestor (AN ses ter) — a parent or relative born before you

aqueduct (AK wih DUKT) — a structure used for carrying running water

archaeologist (AR kee AHL uh jest) — a person who studies past human life by studying artifacts left by ancient people

artifacts(ART eh fakts) — objects made or changed by humans

basilicas (beh SIL ih kez) — early Roman churches or large meeting halls

chariot (CHAIR ee et) — a two- or four-wheeled vehicle of ancient times used in war and in races

chronology (kreh NAHL uh jee) — a science that deals with measuring time and dating events

decay (di KAY) — to break down or decline from a healthy condition

dig (DIG) — a place where excavation takes place

evidence (EV e dens) — anything that can be used as proof

excavated (EK skeh VAYT ed) — having removed earth by digging

gladiators (GLAD ee ay terz) — trained men from ancient Rome who fought each other to the death

GLOSSARY

inhabited (in HAB it ed) — having lived in a place

Paleolithic (PAY lee eh LITH ik) — the earliest and longest period of human history lasting from about 2.5 million years ago to about 10,000 years ago; Old Stone Age

Mesolithic (MEZ eh LITH ik) — a period in European prehistory starting about 8300 BC; Middle Stone Age

mosaic (moe ZAY ik) — a decoration made by placing small pieces of glass or stone together to form a pattern or design

sieve (SIV) — a meshed or screened tool used to separate fine or small materials from larger, coarser ones

temples (TEM pelz) — places used to worship gods and goddesses

tombs (TOOMZ) — places for burial

tradition (treh DISH en) — handing down beliefs and customs by example or word of mouth

FURTHER READING

The Destruction of Pompeii © 1988 Mike Rosen, The Bookwright Press, New York

Rome: Echoes of Imperial Glory © 1994 Editors of Time-Life Books, Time-Life Books, Alexandria, Virginia

Classical Rome © 1993 John D. Clare, Gulliver Books, HBJ Publishers, San Diego, New York, London

The Young Oxford Book of Archaeology ©1997 Norah Moloney, Oxford University Press, NY

Lost Cities © 1997 Paul G. Bahn, Welcome Rain, New York

Ancient Rome, Eyewitness Books ©1990 Simon James, Alfred A. Knopf, Inc., NY

How We Know About the Romans ©1997 John and Louise James, Peter Bedrick Books, New York

Encarta Encyclopedia © 1996 Microsoft Corporation

Grolier Multimedia Encyclopedia ©1998 Grolier Inc.

Mt. Vesuvius
www.volcano.und.nodak.edu/vvdocs/vol_images/img_vesuvius.html

Mt. Vesuvius
www.idt.net/~dobran/

The Imperial Forum Project
www.capitolium.org/

INDEX